Hût Chi B. Répâ

The 20 commandments of success

Success isn't innate, it's built !

Editions VLR

"All rights of reproduction, adaptation and translation, in whole or in part, reserved for all countries. The author or publisher is the sole owner of the rights and responsible for the content of this book. The French Intellectual Property Code prohibits copies or reproductions intended for collective use. Any representation or reproduction in whole or in part by any process whatsoever, without the consent of the author or his successors or assigns, is unlawful and constitutes an infringement under Articles L.335-2 et seq. of the French Intellectual Property Code. "

Please note that the content has been translated using online translation tools; thank you for your understanding.

©Hût Chi B. Repa

Legal deposit: 12/2022
E-mail: info@viselareussite.com
Ean13 : 9798323576067

© *Editions VLR*

*"We all **have** the **tools** for **Success** within us, the important thing is to first **understand** this so that we can then **give** ourselves the **means** to use them to progress and build our own **Success**."*

— Hût Chi B. Répa —

Table of contents

Foreword 7

Commandment 1: Build your own success! 9

2nd Commandment: Use time as an ally! 13

3rd Commandment: Fail and rise again! 17

4th Commandment: You'll make progress no matter what! 21

Commandment 5: Change your bad habits! 25

6th Commandment: Keep your motivation intact! 29

7th Commandment: Thou shalt strive for greatness! 33

8th Commandment: Thou shalt forge a mind of steel! 37

9th Commandment: Thou shalt be bold when necessary! 39

10th Commandment: Thou shalt think long term! 43

11th Commandment: Thou shalt be a leader! 47

12th Commandment: Become a strategist! 51

13th Commandment: Surround yourself with good people! 55

14th Commandment: Thou shalt take care of thy communication! ...59

15th Commandment: Discipline yourself every day! 63

16th Commandment: Thou shalt keep evolving! 67

17th Commandment: Thou shalt challenge thyself!...........................71

18th Commandment: Thou shalt act as a unifier! 75

19th Commandment: Thou shalt not be manipulated! 79

20th Commandment: Thou shalt face thy fears! 83

Conclusion...87

Thanks 91

Foreword

In the digital age of the 21st century, characterized by label **2.0**, constant connection and an unparalleled influx of information, it's becoming imperative to delve deeply into accomplished introspection to grasp the **fundamental principles** that are the cement of our motivation and the pillars of our success.

The primary impetus for this work is none other than the need to enlighten every inquisitive mind on the immutable rules of triumph. It was with sincere humility and deep reflection that I set about writing this book, which sets out to unveil the **20 essential commandments of success.**

Rooted in the hustle and bustle of a world that is digitalizing at dizzying speed, I have drawn from my experiences, both failures and successes, lessons that I feel are essential for anyone seeking to thrive in this age that proudly bears the stigma of **2.0**. The main ambition of this book is to provide you not only with the tools you need, but also with **the interpretive keys** you need to put them to work for your own personal vision.

The Art of War, an undisputed reference on strategy, has always been a source of inspiration for many entrepreneurs and thinkers. Like this masterpiece, the book you are holding in your hands aims to introduce you to **universal**, timeless **principles.** These principles, far from being mere recommendations, aim to establish a profound, even

holistic, understanding of the environment in which you evolve, be it personal or professional.

As the old saying goes, "the times, they are a-changin'". And indeed they do, at a pace that can sometimes confuse us. That's why these **20 commandments are** intended to be your compass, your beacon in the night, to guide you through the twists and turns of a world in perpetual metamorphosis. Their ambition is to help you chart your course, make your mark and **succeed in** every sphere of your existence.

My unshakeable faith in these commandments stems from the concrete results they have generated in my own life and in the lives of the many people I have had the privilege of advising. I'm convinced that, if applied with diligence and perseverance, these principles can transform destinies, elevate ambitions and **create unparalleled success.**

So, dear reader, are you ready to embark on this journey, to let yourself be guided by these **20 commandments**, which aim to revolutionize your perception of success? To immerse yourself in an ocean of wisdom and reflection, to draw the quintessence from it to sculpt the statue of your personal and professional success?

So I enthusiastically and eagerly invite you to turn the page and **dive** into the depths of this book. Let yourself be carried away by the power of these commandments, and discover how they can be the pillars of your own **odyssey to success.** Let's get started together!

Commandment 1: Build your own success!

The quintessence of self-realization: The art of building your own success!

At the heart of our quest for fulfillment lies an undeniable truth: **success is forged**. It's not simply a gift from the stars or the spontaneous product of luck. No, **success is** an edifice, a work of art that we sculpt over time.

We are inundated with stories of prodigies, of geniuses born with extraordinary talents, giving the illusion that success is, for some, a natural companion. However, this perception is deceptive. **Aiming for success** is an art, a discipline that must be acquired. It is certainly not innate.

It's essential to understand that talent, no matter how raw, requires constant polishing. Behind every media prodigy, there are immeasurable hours of practice, repeated failures overcome, sacrifices often invisible to the general public. These stories don't recount the mornings when discouragement weighed more heavily than passion, nor the evenings of isolation devoted to honing their craft away from distractions. They fail to mention that, even for these exceptional beings, **success** is a path strewn with pitfalls, a mountain conquered step by step, with courage and determination.

Self-actualization, in this sense, is accessible to all who are ready to embrace this discipline. It is not the prerogative of a privileged few with innate talent, but rather a promised land for those willing to invest their time, energy and heart. To understand this is to free ourselves from the shackles of intimidation and self-sabotage, to recognize that **we are all capable of sculpting our own masterpiece of success**.

Ultimately, **success** is not a matter of genetic predisposition or cosmic favor. On the contrary, it's a blank canvas on which anyone can paint, a blank book ready to be written. It requires from us an **unshakeable passion**, an **iron will**, and above all, an **inexhaustible faith** in our potential to learn, grow and triumph, whatever the circumstances. In this spirit, success becomes not only an achievable goal, but a true personal work of art, testifying to our unique journey and unwavering commitment to our most cherished aspirations.

When approaching the vast universe of success, it's vital to understand that it reveals itself to us like a jigsaw puzzle. Every piece, every moment of our lives, forms a part of this bigger picture. So, the first commandment to embrace is: **"Build your success yourself."** Waiting for life to serve us our deepest aspirations on a silver platter is a sweet utopia. Success is **hard work**, a mosaic of choices, sacrifices, and relentless effort.

But then, faced with this immense web of possibilities, how do you build your own success?

The first cornerstone is to **define** what success means to you. Is it professional recognition, the gentle whisper of a close-knit family, the tranquillity of financial stability, the treasure of unshakeable health, or perhaps a subtle blend of all these aspirations? It's by digging deep inside ourselves that we unearth our inner treasures, our true motivations.

Once these pillars have been established, it's time to draw up an **action plan**. Think of success as a destination. To get there, we need a map, a compass. This map is made up of **short- and long-term objectives**, milestones that we must reach. Every step is a victory, every achievement a validation of our journey.

Yet, like all travelers, it's crucial to learn to recognize obstacles and distractions. **Setting limits**, learning to say "no" to solicitations that lead us astray, is a crucial skill. Temptation is omnipresent, especially for those whose hearts are set on others. Nevertheless, to sculpt our personal legend, it's fundamental to **prioritize** our needs and aspirations.

However, no construction is free from errors and imperfections. That's why learning and **self-assessment** are the faithful companions of our quest. It's all about cultivating an open mind, gratefully accepting **constructive criticism**, recognizing our weaknesses and drawing life-saving lessons from them. To question ourselves is to nourish our spirit, to enable it to grow.

And above all, there's courage. The courage to take **risks**, to embrace the unknown, to pursue your dreams even when the path becomes obscure. Because success, while requiring planning and strategy, also demands fearless daring.

True success doesn't spring from nothing, nor is it granted by some celestial power. On the contrary, it emanates from a **deliberate will**, a **thirst for success** that burns deep within us, **unshakeable discipline** and the **flexibility** to transform ourselves in the face of obstacles. More than just a result, success is an intimate expedition, a journey strewn with constant learning, leading us to our pinnacles of excellence. Every step forward, every lesson learned from the challenges we face, helps to build our personality and sharpen our know-how. It's the result of our sustained efforts, our ability to overcome setbacks and evolve. Success is thus a **personal quest**, a never-ending exploration of our potential, in which every obstacle we overcome and every skill we acquire brings us a little closer to ultimate fulfillment.

> *"Forge your success with the will of the sculptor, each blow of the hammer shaping your path to the exceptional, in a work of art that only you can create."*

2nd Commandment: Use time as an ally!

The ephemeral and the eternal: Time as the cornerstone of our achievements

In the ceaseless ballet of our existence, one reality remains unshakeable: **time is our most precious commodity**. Like fine sand flowing through an hourglass, every passing second is a golden nugget that, once gone, can never be regained.

Time, unlike material wealth, is a limited and unalterable resource. It is the great silent architect who, with each tick of a clock, shapes our destinies, our failures and our triumphs. Recognizing the inestimable value of time gives us the means to transcend our daily lives, to reach those ethereal heights of our boldest dreams. And yet, in the frenzy of our modern lives, how many of us can claim to have mastered this ephemeral treasure? Drowning in a sea of tasks, demands and distractions, we often find ourselves exhausted, our souls in pain, lamenting the time we've lost.

So it's imperative that we **re-enchant our relationship with time**. So how do we transform this impetuous torrent into a benevolent ally, an accomplice to our ambitions?

First, the art of **planning**. Every morning, before the sun sets its first light on the horizon, give yourself a sacred moment of reflection. In the quiet of these moments, **draw up a list of** your obligations, whether professional or intimate. This daily cartography will give you a clear vision, an aerial perspective of your day, enabling you to isolate what is vital from what is superfluous.

Then, **prioritizing** is the key. Among the constellations of activities that populate your universe, certain stars shine with a particular brilliance, dictating the pace of your steps. Identify them. These crucial tasks, these cardinal missions, must be honored first and foremost. They are the foundation, the central pillar on which your success is built.

However, skilfully navigating the labyrinth of time also requires vigilance against the sirens of **distraction**. These insidious distractions creep into our routines, diluting our concentration and scattering our energies. Be disciplined: learn to disconnect, to erect barriers against these parasites. In a hyper-connected world, define sanctuaries of silence, havens of peace where your mind can, sheltered from the storms, focus on what's essential.

But never underestimate the regenerative power of **breaks**. In the frantic race towards our goals, it's sometimes salutary to stop, breathe and contemplate the beauty that surrounds us. These interludes are oases, sources of inspiration where the mind can recharge and revitalize itself.

The digital age, with its procession of innovations, provides us with a panoply of **time management tools**. Applications, software, collaborative platforms: explore these marvels and adopt the ones that resonate with your needs and aspirations. They can be real compasses in your quest for efficiency.

In conclusion, treating **time as a precious commodity** is not just a philosophy; it's a categorical imperative for anyone wishing to leave their mark on the marble of history. Every tick is an invitation, a challenge to honor our potential, to sculpt a future that lives up to our wildest dreams. When we learn to dance with time, to respect it, to cherish it, then and only then do we unlock the doors to infinite possibilities.

"Let time be your ally in this quest. Every moment is an opportunity, every moment a stone to build your path to success."

3rd Commandment: Fail and rise again!

Unravelling the riddle of failure: Towards the metamorphosis of our flaws

Life, this epic of triumph and disillusionment, is punctuated by moments of glory, but also by moments when everything seems to fall apart. It is in this often painful context that the true nature of **failure is** revealed. At first glance, failure is a feeling of overwhelm, defeat and even humiliation. Yet, when we take a closer look, **failure is the primary source of success**. It offers us, hidden beneath its sometimes cruel features, a window onto the immensity of our unexplored potential.

If we were asked to list the inescapable commandments that dictate the course of our lives, **the third commandment** would unquestionably emerge: "Consider every failure as the preamble to a great success". It's a maxim of dazzling relevance, especially in the prism of our contemporary society.

We live in a world that magnifies perfection, that sets up unattainable figures as models, and that simultaneously castigates those who stumble, those who dare to stray from the beaten track to forge their own paths. In this frantic quest for success, we forget that **failure is inevitable**, and above all that it is intrinsic to the construction of our beings.

Realizing that every failure is a fundamental building block on our path to success is a lesson that transcends the ages. Indeed, every setback, every obstacle overcome, offers us **an opportunity to** question ourselves, to refine our understanding of the worlds around us, and to revisit our strategies.

Obviously, admitting failure, welcoming it with open arms and transmuting it into a propulsive force can be a daunting task. It requires profound humility, an ability to **appreciate** our shortcomings as much as our successes. But this process is imperative, for it is through our falls, our abrasions, that we forge our **resilience**.

History is littered with illustrious figures whose lives, littered with pitfalls, are living proof that downfalls are only ephemeral, and that they are often the prelude to great flights. **Steve Jobs**, an icon of innovation, experienced the anguish of redundancy, the anguish of seeing his dream crumble. But it was this dark period that was the catalyst for a dazzling resurrection, culminating in the creation of Apple, that technological titan. As for **J.K. Rowling,** her journey to fame was littered with bitter failures, rejection letters and incomprehension. Yet each rejection strengthened her resolve, sharpened her pen, and led her to give birth to the fantastic world of Harry Potter, the saga that has fired the imagination of millions.

Failure, that mysterious companion on the road, is not a fatality, an irrevocable sentence. It is a **stage**, a master who, through his sometimes bitter lessons, prepares us for the heights of success. And even if the temptation to give up is great, we must remember that behind every shadow lies a light, behind every night a dawn.

Ultimately, it's up to us, the architects of our destinies, to choose how to interpret our setbacks. Will they be chains that shackle us, or springboards to as-yet unimagined horizons? **The next time failure comes knocking at your door**, welcome it as an old friend, a mentor, and know that it is only there to show you the way to even greater triumphs.

> *"In the book of life, failure is just one chapter, but getting back up is the real story. Every fall is a lesson, every rise a victory over oneself."*

4th Commandment: You'll make progress no matter what!

Invaluable skills: The matrix of your professional and personal ascension

As we go through the tapestry of talents and aptitudes that each individual possesses, we often marvel at the multitude of **skills that** each of us holds. These skills, as varied as they may be, constitute an intangible treasure, an intrinsic capital that forges our professional identity. They are, without a shadow of a doubt, **your intangible advantage**. These faculties, these distinctive skills, are the pillars on which any potential for excellence rests.

In the universal doctrine of personal and professional fulfillment, if there were to be a list of commandments, the **fourth commandment** would unquestionably be: "Thou shalt thrive by embracing constant evolution, never giving in to the temptation to give up". A precept which, at first glance, might appear ambiguous, but which, in its essence, exhorts us to a relentless quest for progress, whatever the turbulence of life.

Life's path is a winding one, marked by victories, defeats, hopes and disappointments. But one constant remains unshakeable: **progress is vital**. Giving up is not an option. Every trial, every obstacle, every pain hides a lesson, a teaching that nourishes our wisdom and refines our strategy.

The sanctuary of your **skills** is your citadel. These skills, shaped by time, effort and passion, are the keys that open the doors of opportunity, transforming dreams into tangible realities. These skills can become the springboard, the **decisive catalyst**, propelling you to unexplored heights.

Nurturing, nurturing and cultivating these skills becomes, therefore, a sacrosanct mission. The modern world offers a plethora of means to achieve this - **training**, practical apprenticeships, specialized literature, seminars, workshops, and more. The thirst for learning must be unquenchable, because every drop of accumulated knowledge enriches your competitive arsenal.

With this in mind, it's essential to bring these skills to light and put them into action. Whether personal initiatives, collaborative projects or professional explorations, each experience is a canvas on which your skills leave their mark. By setting yourself apart, by bringing your unique **added value**, you establish your brand, your inimitable signature.

Developing and refining your skills has another, often underestimated, benefit: the anchoring of robust **self-confidence.** As you gain greater mastery of your field and deepen your know-how, you become more self-assured and daring. This renewed confidence is the driving force that encourages you to take bold initiatives, to embrace previously daunting challenges.

What's more, in an age where routine and monotony can easily creep in, the continuous enrichment of your skills is the balm that keeps you

motivated and passionate. By learning and evolving, every day is a new day, a horizon that promises new adventures and new quests.

Never forget this universal truth: **your skills** are the mirror of your potential, the compass that guides you towards excellence. In the whirlwinds of life, in the storms of challenges, always remember the power that lies within you. Whatever the circumstances, whatever the headwinds, **never give up**. Within you lies an immeasurable strength, a light that's just waiting to shine.

> *"Whatever the trials and tribulations along the way, your forward march is inevitable. Every trial is just another step towards your fulfillment."*

Commandment 5: Change your bad habits!

Habits: the silent architects of our destiny

Human nature is a complex and fascinating web of **traditions**, **reflexes** and **automatisms** which, together, sculpt the very nature of our daily lives. At the heart of this complexity are our **habits**. From trivial rituals to more elaborate actions, these routines reflect our character, our history and our aspirations.

Imagine for a moment the architecture of a cathedral: each stone, each pillar, each vault is carefully placed, part of a much larger structure. **Habits** are to our psyche what these stones are to the cathedral: structural elements on which the integrity of our being rests. They become, over time, actions so deeply rooted that they manifest themselves without thought, like reflexes.

In the quest for personal development, the **Fifth Commandment** stands out as a compass guiding us to evaluate and, if necessary, reform these habits. But if these rituals are so deeply ingrained, why and how should we change them?

To answer this question, we need to delve into the mechanics of the mind. The **brain, in all** its splendid ingenuity, is an optimization machine. It establishes routines to save energy and perform tasks with maximum efficiency. But sometimes, what's efficient isn't always optimal for our well-being or personal fulfillment. A habit that once seemed beneficial can turn into a burden, or worse, a chain.

The question then arises: **how can we reorient** this formidable machine that is the brain to adopt new routines?

The process is as demanding as it is rewarding. The first step is always **recognition**. Like an artist evaluating a canvas, identify that habit that needs transformation. This process requires deep introspection, brutal honesty and a willingness to see beyond the surface.

Once identified, the second step is to **devise a strategy**. If the old habit was a well-marked road, the new one is a barely perceptible path that needs to be created. To guide this process, the use of **triggers** or reminders, such as notes on a desk or an alarm, can be crucial.

The real test, however, is **implementation**. Like a sculptor carving a stone, every day is an opportunity to reinforce this new habit. It's natural to encounter resistance, moments of weakness, but the key is **perseverance**.

Never neglect the power of **reward**. Like a traveler enjoying an oasis after a long journey, give yourself moments of gratification for each milestone reached. These rewards, big or small, are the fuel that fuels motivation.

It's crucial to remember that each individual is a universe unto itself, with its own laws and dynamics. Methods that work for one may not work for another. But in this quest to transform habits, one constant remains: **patience**. Time, combined with determination, shapes mountains.

The mission, though titanic, has inestimable repercussions. By modifying a single habit, a whole part of our existence is redefined, offering greater harmony of **body** and **mind**. And on this journey, never forget that every effort, every failure, every success is a step towards building a more fulfilled version of yourself.

> *"Like a gardener uprooting weeds, you'll cultivate fertile ground for flourishing by pulling out your bad habits. Every effort is a seed planted for a better life."*

6th Commandment: Keep your motivation intact!

The inner flame: Passion as the key to perseverance

At the heart of the human journey, between starry-eyed aspirations and the soil of experience where our feet find their anchorage, lies an intrinsic force - an inner compass, guiding us through life's labyrinths. This compass is our **motivation**. It doesn't just light the way; it embodies the fire that burns within us, driving us over mountains and valleys to reach our desired horizons.

However, as every traveler knows, the road is often strewn with **pitfalls**. How then, in the face of these storms and trials, do we stay the course? How do we ensure that the flame of our motivation is not extinguished in the cold wind of doubt or the driving rain of failure?

One of the answers to these age-old questions lies in a concept as old as humanity itself: **passion**. When we **devote ourselves to** a task, a project, or even a life with burning passion, every action becomes a symphony, every obstacle a challenge to be overcome with renewed ardor. Passion is that spark which, when it ignites our being, transforms the most arduous tasks into exhilarating quests.

The famous adage "Love what you do, and you'll never have to work a day in your life" illustrates this principle perfectly. **Loving what we do, being passionate about it**, gives our motivation a raison d'être, making it both robust in the face of storms and flexible in the face of unforeseen detours.

To keep this passion alive, and the motivation it fuels unwavering, it's essential to adopt a judicious **strategy. This is** where the notion of **goals** comes in.

Choosing the right lenses is a delicate process. Like an artist choosing his colors, you need to know how to balance **ambition** and **realism**. Goals that are too distant or unrealistic risk casting a shadow over motivation, making it unattainable and therefore discouraging. Conversely, goals that are too easy can extinguish the flame of passion, making it monotonous. So it's crucial to choose **milestones** that, while challenging, remain within our grasp.

Once these objectives have been established, the journey really begins. And here, the "step-by-step" strategy comes into its own. Let's imagine a mountain for a moment. If we focus solely on the distant summit, discouragement can set in. However, by **breaking up** the ascent, celebrating each small success, each step taken, the summit becomes progressively closer, and the climb becomes a series of jubilant victories.

The challenge of keeping **motivation** intact boils down to a few key principles. First and foremost, we must embrace our **passion**, the flame that lights up our aspirations. Next, it's crucial to **set** sound objectives, the beacons that will guide our journey. Finally, we must approach each challenge "step by step", savoring every success, no matter how small.

The journey is perhaps more precious than the destination. It's on this journey that we discover ourselves, grow and shape our destiny. Motivation and passion, these two forces combined, become the wind beneath our wings, propelling us to ever greater heights.

And, dear reader, in the hope that these words have enlightened your path, I invite you to share this reflection with others, and to enrich this dialogue with your own experiences and reflections.

"Perseverance forges dreams, but it's undiminished motivation that paves the way to the stars."

7th Commandment: Thou shalt strive for greatness!

Man's supreme drive: Inordinate ambition, the key to success

On the threshold of existence, each individual, equipped with dreams and passions, steps into the arena of the world, equipped with his or her talents and armed with determination. Yet, amidst this mosaic of souls, only a few seem to stand out, driven by an inner force both mysterious and irresistible: **overweening ambition**.

Strangely enough, this ambition, often judged pejoratively, proves to be a veritable catalyst for those who embrace it. It is the lantern illuminating their winding paths, the wind filling their sails during uncertain crossings, and the anchor holding them in place against the temptation of abandonment.

But what about the powerful yet controversial notion of **ambition**?

Dig deeper and you'll discover that ambition isn't simply a thirst for success or a frantic quest for recognition. It is, in fact, the deep-seated desire to **leave a mark**, to make a memorable contribution to the world, be it artistic, scientific, humanitarian or otherwise. Ambition is that inner compass which, if properly calibrated, can guide us to unsuspected heights.

However, it would be a mistake to be content with modest ambition. **Excessive ambition** offers the unique ability to push back boundaries, explore the unknown and transcend the ordinary. It urges the individual to never be satisfied with the status quo, to question, to innovate and, above all, to continually **reinvent** himself.

Nevertheless, it would be naïve not to approach ambition without a word of warning. This powerful energy, misdirected, can lead to excesses such as selfishness, arrogance and blindness. For ambition to be beneficial, it must be balanced by humility, respect and a genuine **ethical conscience**.

To **nurture** and **cultivate** this boundless ambition, several steps can be taken. First and foremost, **defining objectives is** the cornerstone. These objectives, while clear and precise, must be bold enough to destabilize, challenge and encourage thinking outside the box.

The importance of a social circle cannot be overlooked. Surrounding yourself with people who share the same thirst for excellence, the same audacity, can be an invaluable source of inspiration. They become **allies** on this path strewn with pitfalls, offering support, encouragement and sometimes different perspectives to overcome challenges.

Boldness, the ability to take calculated risks, is also a cornerstone of this ambition. For, as the saying goes: "Nothing ventured, nothing gained". So we need to be adventurous and daring, but also prepared and resilient.

Perseverance, that virtue which constantly reminds us that the road to greatness is long and strewn with obstacles, proves to be the final link in this chain. Ambition, no matter how great, doesn't materialize with a snap of the fingers. It takes time, patience, determination and, above all, unshakeable faith in one's abilities and destiny.

Inordinate ambition is not simply a folly of grandeur, but a philosophy, a way of life which, if embraced with wisdom and discernment, can open the door to extraordinary achievements. It is a reminder that man, when freed from the shackles of mediocrity, can achieve prodigies, and that everyone, regardless of origin or situation, carries within him a spark capable of setting the world ablaze.

> *"He who aims for the stars touches the top of the world, for it is in the immensity of our ambitions that lies the key to extraordinary achievements."*

8th Commandment: Thou shalt forge a mind of steel!

The sanctuary of the spirit: Forging a mind of steel through the quest for excellence

In the frenetic whirl of modern life, there is a universal truth that the **8th commandment** highlights: the imperative need to **work one's mind** with unparalleled relentlessness. Like a sculptor shaping his rough stone, the individual must chisel his mind, aiming for excellence to arm himself in the face of adversity.

But what is the secret of this indomitable mind, this inner strength that seems to propel certain individuals to the top, even when the winds are against them?

The first and most important step is to **define your objectives**. Every great journey requires a map, and our quest for mental excellence is no exception. We need to set out a clear path, illuminating our journey with precise markers. To be effective, these goals must combine ambition and **realism**. They must be audacious, stimulating enthusiasm, while remaining anchored in the realm of the possible, thus ensuring long-term motivation.

But simply setting goals is not enough. **Training is** fundamental. Just as a musician rehearses his scales or an athlete refines his techniques, the individual in search of a mind of steel must practice regularly. Whether through **meditation**, which sharpens concentration and soothes torment, **reading**, which broadens horizons and nourishes reflection, or **visualization**, that powerful technique of mental immersion in the future realization of our ambitions.

However, danger lurks at every turn: doubt, discouragement, negativity. Here, it's crucial to **cultivate a positive attitude**, to root ourselves in beliefs that lift us up. Optimism, far from being naïve, is a formidable weapon against adversity. Constantly reminding ourselves of past successes, surrounding ourselves with inspiring role models and repeating positive affirmations are all strategies for strengthening this mental shield.

Paradoxically, in the midst of this relentless quest, it's essential to learn **moderation** and **set limits**. Just as an athlete avoids overtraining, the mental worker needs to know when to say no, when to take it easy. It's in this delicate balance that the secret of mental longevity lies, preserving the inner flame from outer blasts.

The quest for a **mind of steel** doesn't just happen. It's the fruit of a thoughtful, structured approach, requiring determination and discipline. It is through scrupulous adherence to these precepts that we can hope to reach this ideal, this summit where the spirit, unshaken, serenely contemplates the storms of life. Such a conquest certainly requires sacrifice, but it offers in return an inner strength, serenity and self-confidence that are priceless.

> *"In the forge of adversity, an indomitable spirit is tempered, sculpting a mind of steel, invincible against the storms of fate."*

9th Commandment: Thou shalt be bold when necessary!

The audacity revolution: The bright flame of inner courage

Boldness is not just a quality. It is a compass that guides, a fire that animates and a shield that protects. An individual's worth is not measured by his or her ability to follow established norms, but rather by his or her ability to challenge the status quo with unwavering resolve. This is underlined by the **9th Commandment**: "*Thou shalt be bold when necessary*", a precept that illuminates the path to greatness.

The real question is: what is audacity, that much-glorified component, and how do we embody it in our tumultuous lives? It is the **very definition of courage**, the ability to defy adversity, to stand up to doubt and embrace the unknown with unbridled passion. It is the refusal of stagnation, the antidote to complacency.

However, let's not confuse boldness with recklessness. Bold action is a **measured act**, a calculated risk. It is the fruit of **profound self-confidence** and an acute awareness of one's capabilities. It requires mental preparation, anticipation of eventualities and unfailing determination. Boldness is the art of stepping out of one's **comfort zone**, plunging into the unknown while being aware of the implications.

Boldness is best illustrated by its ability to **transform dreams into tangible realities**. It opens doors, moves mountains, creates opportunities where none existed before. Boldness is the North Star that guides us towards uncharted horizons, the energy that breaks the shackles of fear and launches us on an exhilarating adventure.

However, being bold is an art that requires refinement. For some, it may come naturally, but for most, it requires **training**. So how do you develop that bold, intrepid courage?

Confronting your fears is the first step. Fear is an illusory obstacle, often amplified by our imagination. By facing up to it, we realize that the shadows that frightened us were merely mirages.

Taking calculated risks is essential. It's not about acting rashly, but assessing situations and moving forward with a strategy in mind.

Listening to your instincts is an underestimated weapon. Very often, our intuition, that inner voice, knows what's good for us, even if it defies logic.

Developing courage is fundamental. You have to put yourself to the test, confront your limits and push them back.

Practicing boldness is a must. Like a muscle, it gets stronger with use. Look for opportunities to challenge your routine, to take initiative, to innovate.

Boldness is not the absence of fear, but rather the recognition that something else is more important than fear. It's the **refreshing breeze** that blows away clouds of doubt, the spark that ignites passion.

Of course, daring has its challenges. There will be mistakes, missteps. But every mistake is a **valuable lesson**, a step towards mastery. The most important thing is never to give up, to stay the course with **unshakeable determination**.

Finally, **audacity is a journey**, a perpetual quest for excellence. It's a call to action, a cry from the heart. It is the key to personal fulfillment, the sesame to great success. In an age when conformity is often the norm, audacity is the wind of revolution that changes everything. Embrace it, cherish it, and watch the world open up before you.

> *"Boldness at the right moment is the brush that paints destiny in vivid colors, for it is by daring that we trace the paths of the impossible."*

10th Commandment: Thou shalt think long term!

The art of anticipation: Navigating between dreams and reality

Anticipating the future is a delicate exercise, requiring both audacity and discernment. Throughout the ages, mankind has distinguished itself by its ability to imagine distant horizons, to **foresee** tomorrow and to **create** a future that lives up to its aspirations. In the labyrinthine complexity of our lives, how do we manage to see beyond the end of our noses, spot golden **opportunities** and dodge abyssal chasms?

Long-term thinking is a skill that few have mastered, a key that opens the door to starry destinies. Far beyond mere mental projection, it evokes a deep understanding of oneself, a meticulous analysis of one's environment and a **clear vision of** where one wants to end up. We live in an effervescent age, where the hustle and bustle of everyday life assails us, and every moment holds a multitude of emergencies. The ability to free one's gaze from the mirages of the moment, and lift it towards the constellations of tomorrow, is more than a talent, it's a **vocation**.

First and foremost, it's important to **sound out your soul**. What is the nature of your desires? Where do you want to be in a decade? What mountains do you long to climb, what seas do you wish to sail? By asking yourself these fundamental questions, you shape the contours of your **destiny**.

Then forge your path by imagining each step. Like a maestro composing a symphony, you need to anticipate every note, every pause, every crescendo. This is the **preparation** phase, where every detail counts. Draw up a strategic plan, establish milestones against which you can measure your progress, and identify the resources - human, financial and time - that are essential to making your odyssey a reality.

The world is full of **opportunities**. They are hidden in the interstices of everyday life, in chance encounters and unexpected challenges. They can take the form of innovative training courses, unexpected job offers or life-changing experiences. **Stay alert**, because luck favours a prepared mind.

But beware! Every journey has its **pitfalls**. Distractions are omnipresent, ready to divert the traveler from his chosen path. Bad habits, like sirens, sing their bewitching melody to keep you from your ultimate goal. **Discipline**, that inner watchdog, must remain alert, scanning the horizon to keep you on the right path.

The 10th Commandment - a cornerstone of ancient wisdom - exhorts us to adopt this far-sighted vision, to prepare our boat for storms and calm waters, to tirelessly seek **opportunities** and guard against **pitfalls**.

In short, navigating life's vast ocean requires a well-drawn map, a precise compass and a guiding star. This trident of success - **thinking long term, imagining** and **creating** - is your assurance of a successful crossing. Follow this compass, and the treasure of a fulfilled life, rich in meaning and satisfaction, awaits you in port.

> *"Tomorrow's dreams are woven into today's long-term thinking, for it's by looking beyond the horizon that we discover the promising lands of the future."*

11th Commandment: Thou shalt be a leader!

The leadership manifesto: sculpting your destiny by illuminating that of others

In the vast echoes of humanity, **the call of leadership is** heard. It echoes in the souls of those ready to take the lead, **embrace responsibility**, and sketch out a collective vision. *You are a leader, not a follower.* This propels you far beyond mere action; it confers on you the role of **luminary**, one who enlightens, inspires, and who, through his actions and words, shapes a brighter future.

Let's delve deeper into this quest for authentic leadership.

Leaders are distinguished by a unique alchemy of innate and acquired qualities. Yes, there are **natural leaders** who seem to be endowed with a supernatural ability to enthuse the troops. These individuals have a natural charisma, a presence that captivates and inspires. However, leadership is far more complex than this single trait. It's a subtle blend of active listening, **insightful communication**, and relentless **adaptability** to the changing needs of the team they guide.

In the face of adversity, the leader demonstrates **unwavering decisiveness**, confidently cutting through the twists and turns of ambiguous choices and multiple scenarios. He is that pillar of **courage** and **determination** where others might falter, daring bold gambles when the situation calls for it, and adopting a thoughtful stance when caution is called for.

Leadership doesn't stop there. It requires intense **motivation**, and the ability to inspire that same motivation in others. Imagine a work environment where every individual feels valued, where every effort is recognized, where trust reigns, and where **mutual respect** is the cornerstone of interactions. This is the world the leader creates, by instilling a **culture of recognition** and fostering a spirit of collaboration that transcends individuality.

As a **guide,** the leader offers clear direction, illuminating the way ahead while arming his team with the tools needed to navigate through challenges. He is that **moral and professional compass**, embodying ethics and excellence, standing on the front line, ready to take the blows while protecting those he leads.

This journey to the heart of authentic leadership is not for the fainthearted. It requires deep introspection, a thirst for continuous improvement, and a **passion** for the common good. Leadership is demanding, but it's also a deeply **rewarding** path. By forging the success of his team, the leader sculpts his own epic.

And so, when trials arise, when doubts invade, and the path seems uncertain, remember this truth: *You are a leader, a figure who transcends the role of mere participant. You are called to guide, to illuminate, to serve as an example.* Embrace this mission, for in elevating others, you elevate yourself.

"In every decision, in every gesture, lies the essence of leadership; to behave as a leader is to illuminate dark paths with the light of example."

12th Commandment: Become a strategist!

The art of strategy: sculpting your way to eminence

At the heart of history's great achievements, behind every visionary and every disruptive innovation, lies a universal constant: **strategy**. It is the embodiment of preparation, the crystallization of reflection, the reflection of ambition. *You* are the strategy, the catalyst of this transformation.

The **12th Commandment** of Operational Excellence states a profound truth: *Put on the strategist's outfit*. Is it not the most essential armor in the arena of contemporary success? It's an invitation to develop a **winning strategy** that transcends mere desire, to become a precise instrument that shapes destinies and empires.

But what's at the heart of this triumphant strategy?
Of course, there is no universal elixir, no magic formula that will guarantee success. However, the strategic creation process is based on **immutable principles** which, once mastered, pave the way to excellence.

The adventure begins with a clear definition of **your objectives**. What is the North Star that guides your ship through the stormy waters of the marketplace? What is the vision that burns in your eyes and drives you to excel? Rigorous introspection is imperative. Arm yourself with your aspirations, refine them, quantify them, until they become unshakeable beacons in your quest.

Knowledge and **insight** are the twins of the strategist. Understanding the ecology of your field - be it a business, an art project, a political campaign - is essential. What are the strengths that set you apart, the weaknesses that hinder you? Who are the rivals sharing your arena, and what movements are they sketching out in the shadows? What unexplored opportunities lurk on the horizon, and what threats could emerge from the storm? SWOT (Strengths, Weaknesses, Opportunities, Threats) analysis is an invaluable prism for crystallizing this reflection.

But a strategy, no matter how brilliant, remains sterile without **execution**. It must be anchored in a robust methodology. It's essential to design a meticulous **action plan**, a roadmap that details every step, every milestone, every resource. But the sea of business is changeable, and your compass must be complemented by modern navigational instruments. Establish rigorous **monitoring** and **control** mechanisms, beacons that ensure the relevance of your trajectory, and enable you to adjust course if necessary.

The art of the strategist is not just a series of techniques or methodologies. It's a **philosophy**, a way of looking at the world. Every decision, every action, every alliance is taken in the wake of this grand vision. It's a profound commitment, a constant quest to harmonize inner aspirations with the realities of the outside world.

Ultimately, to embrace the role of strategist is to sculpt one's destiny. It's choosing to be the master of your ship rather than leaving it to the mercy of fickle winds. It's a delicate dance between **preparation** and **adaptability**, **vision** and **action**.

So, as the world bubbles with challenges and opportunities, as uncertainty hovers like a hawk ready to swoop down on its prey, remember this mantra: *Get ready. Forge your winning strategy.* The future is yours.

"A strategist's vision is a beacon in the night, guiding to victory not by force, but by intelligence and precision of choice."

13th Commandment: Surround yourself with good people!

The mosaic of relationships: Be the central sun of your relational Universe

In the vast theater of life, where each actor plays a crucial role, it's imperative to realize that *you are the sun, around which the planets of your relationships revolve*. **You influence those around you, not the other way around!** Your light, your energy, determines the quality of the links you forge and the harmony of your social galaxy.

The **13th Commandment,** far from being self-evident, holds within it an ancestral wisdom. It reminds us that the choice of protagonists in our personal saga is not a matter of chance, but a carefully considered decision. For, inevitably, **we are all shaped by our surroundings**. Just as iron is shaped by the blacksmith's hammer, our minds and souls are shaped by the influences that surround us.

But if we look at the complexity of human relationships, one question emerges: How do we discern the precious metal from the dross? How can we distinguish the shining stars from the black holes in our relational firmament?

The answer to this question lies first and foremost in **sincere introspection**. By anchoring ourselves in our own essence, by listening to those inner murmurs, we can detect the dissonances, those discordant notes that disturb our inner melody. When a presence arouses doubt, anxiety or simple discomfort in us, it may be time to reassess its place in our constellation.

But vigilance is not enough. It's essential to **nurture those relationships** that bring us warmth, joy and vitality. By their very presence, they brighten our days, recharging our emotional batteries and spurring us on to surpass ourselves.

The team that surrounds us is the cornerstone of our edifice. Whether it's a blood sibling - the family, the sacred circle of friendship, or the professional network, this benevolent army represents our shield, our anchor in stormy waters. **Trusting** these sentinels, these guardians of our integrity, is more than a choice, it's a necessity. Their unwavering support, unique perspective and unconditional love form the solid fabric on which our story is woven.

It's just as important to protect ourselves from **harmful influences**. Worrying spirits, hardened pessimists, or simply those who, by their actions and words, seek to erode our esteem. It's not a question of animosity, but of an elegant distance that preserves the integrity of our inner world.

The journey towards the idealized self is a winding one, paved with uncertainties and challenges. But with a **solid team**, a hand-picked entourage, every ordeal becomes a step towards ascension. By placing people who uplift us at the center of our universe, we are not only assured of an upward trajectory, we also become beacons for those seeking their own path.

The delicate dance of human relationships requires both discernment and commitment. **Surrounding yourself wisely means** building a fortress of well-being and fulfillment. It means equipping ourselves with an arsenal to conquer the heights of our aspirations and refusing to be overwhelmed by the waves of doubts and fears.

Like a finely assembled mosaic, where each tessera has been chosen for its color, shape and texture, our surroundings compose the living tableau of our existence. Let's ensure that each piece reflects the light, beauty and strength we wish to radiate within and around us.

> *"To choose your companions is to build the foundations of your destiny; to surround yourself with good people is to sow the seeds of success in the garden of your life."*

14th Commandment: Thou shalt take care of thy communication!

The subtle art of communication: The silent power of the spoken and unspoken word

In the complex ballet of human relationships, if there's one skill that stands like a majestic pillar, it's the ability to **communicate**. Like a delicate but resilient spider's web, it weaves the bonds between us, building bridges where abysses threaten to separate us. **Knowing how to lead is knowing how to communicate**. But more than that, it means embracing the fundamental truth that *communication is an art*.

The **14th Commandment is** not only thought-provoking, it is a universal maxim to which everyone, whatever their status, should bow. Every word we speak, every gesture we make, carries with it a weight, a meaning, a message.

The professional scene, with its ceaseless challenges and ever-changing dynamics, amplifies the importance of this communication. An effective **leader** is not only one who gives clear directives, but also one who knows how to listen, interpret and adapt. Each team member is a unique instrument; together, they compose a symphony. For this melody to be harmonious, the communication score must be impeccable.

But this magic of communication is not limited to the corporate arena. It infuses every fragment of our existence. **Practicing positive**

communication is like caressing the soul with carefully chosen words. Where criticism and judgment weave barbed wire through the gardens of our relationships, communication imbued with empathy and respect sows seeds of understanding and harmony.

This journey towards communicative excellence, however, is not without its pitfalls. It requires vigilance, introspection and, above all, **practice**. It invites us to :
- **Listening with authenticity**, offering our interlocutor a space of respect and understanding.
- Cultivate **clarity** and **conciseness**, serving up our ideas with precise words like a conductor guides his troupe with precision.
- Move away from sterile criticism to embrace **constructive solutions**, like an artist choosing bright colors for a painting.
- Wear a veil of **empathy**, immersing yourself in the deep waters of the other person's emotions and points of view.
- Be **true to yourself**. In a world where masks often outnumber faces, showing your true self is both a challenge and a liberation.

Beyond words, **non-verbal communication** dances around us like silent butterflies carrying messages. Our eyes, our hands, the cadence of our voice - all whisper secrets as powerful as the spoken word. They are the discreet accomplices of our intentions, and by mastering them, we add nuances to our communicative palette.

Ultimately, to embrace the art of communication is to recognize its transformative **power.** It's a tool, a weapon, a gift. By polishing it, adapting it, respecting it, we open doors to deeper relationships, mutual understanding and personal and collective growth.

So, at a time when words are often lost in the tumult of our noisy age, let's choose to give them meaning, direction and purpose. **Let's master the art of communication**, because through it, we define not only who we are, but also the world we want to live in.

> *"Speech is the bridge between souls; taking care of your communication means building golden bridges over which ideas and hearts can meet."*

15th Commandment: Discipline yourself every day!

The inner quest: Taming your being in a world of chaos

Human existence is a whirlwind of **emotions**, **sensations** and **experiences**. It evokes the image of a tumultuous ocean, where every wave is an emotion, every current an event, every tide a chapter in life. And just as a sailor needs to master the elements to navigate successfully, we as individuals need to **master our emotions** to steer the boat of our existence.

"Learn to tame your emotions! You're in the driver's seat of your life." These words, like a lighthouse in the darkness, illuminate the path ahead. Every individual carries within them the **15th Commandment**, this guideline, sometimes enigmatic, but whose wisdom is unshakeable.

At first sight, this commandment may seem as dizzying as climbing a mountain. And yet, just as every summit conquered reveals panoramas of unsuspected beauty, this precept conceals within it the key to **personal fulfillment**.

So how do you set off on this quest for yourself with confidence and determination?
It's not simply a matter of sailing by sight or letting ourselves be tossed about by the waves of life. It's imperative to **clearly define our objectives**, breaking them down into tangible, measurable steps. This

gives us a clear vision and a roadmap, an itinerary for our inner journey.

Then comes the need for **discipline**. A term that can be intimidating, even frightening, but which in reality is the silent accomplice of all success. It's essential to carve out a routine, a series of actions and rituals which, repeated with devotion, forge our character and hone our resilience. Rising at dawn to greet the new day, devoting moments to movement and exercise, immersing oneself in the abyss of silence through **meditation** - these are all practices which, though simple, can transform an existence.

But beyond our actions, it's our inner temple, our **body**, that requires constant, dedicated attention. Food, the essence that nourishes our cells, must be chosen with care. Exercise, the dance that makes every muscle and joint vibrate, must be a celebration, not a chore. Sleep, that nocturnal journey where the spirit rests and regenerates, must be sacred.

However, the quest would not be complete without mentioning the sea of **emotions** that roars within us. They are, at times, our best allies and, at others, our most formidable adversaries. **Taming these emotions** means recognizing them, understanding them, and above all, giving them the place they deserve. It's not a question of repressing them, but of channeling them, transforming them into creative energy.

And, in this whirlwind of emotions and actions, let's never forget that **we are the undisputed masters of our own destiny**. External influences, however powerful, are mere whispers in the face of the resounding voice of our will. Every decision we make, every step we take, every mistake we make is an opportunity to learn, to grow and to transcend ourselves.

Embracing the **15th Commandment** is not a simple task, but a true priesthood. By caring for our inner temple, wisely navigating the seas of our emotions, and taking firm control of the rudder of our lives, we don't just live; we evolve, we shine, we triumph. It's up to us to pursue this quest with zeal, for at the end of the road lies the most fulfilled, authentic and luminous version of ourselves.

"Daily discipline is the foundation on which the edifice of excellence is built, each day polished by effort becomes a jewel in the crown of success."

16th Commandment: Thou shalt keep evolving!

The relentless quest for knowledge: Towards perpetual evolution

In the depths of human history, evolution has always been the common thread that has guided our steps, sometimes gropingly, sometimes confidently. It's not just a genetic directive, but a profound incentive, inscribed in our soul and spirit, urging us never to remain static, but always to seek, aspire and desire more. **Learn, live, evolve!** These three words, though simple, resonate with immeasurable force, tracing a guideline for a life of fulfillment.

Throughout the ages, our ability to learn and adapt has been one of the most defining characteristics of the human species. Insatiable curiosity, this thirst for knowledge, has led the great thinkers of every age to push back the boundaries of our understanding, paving the way for major advances in every field, from science to art to philosophy. Every **day that** passes, every moment of reflection, every moment of curiosity is an opportunity. A chance to **learn**, to embrace the new, to understand the world and shape our place in it.

Living is much more than just breathing. It's feeling every vibration, every emotion, every joy and every sorrow. It's confronting our challenges, facing our fears, celebrating our triumphs and learning from our failures. Life is a tumultuous journey, a sea of uncertainty, but it's also fertile ground for growth, transformation and evolution. Every experience, every interaction, every choice is a step towards a better version of ourselves. It is this very essence that drives us to continue, to seek, to desire, to **evolve**.

But how can we ensure that we don't **stagnate** in this quest for perpetual evolution?

Stagnation is the antithesis of evolution. It manifests itself when we wallow in routine, avoid change and shun novelty. To avoid this pitfall, we must continually question ourselves, challenge established norms, seek new perspectives and open up to unexplored paradigms.

There are several strategies you can adopt. First, cultivate an unwavering **curiosity**. In an ever-changing world, the act of learning becomes a necessity, whether through reading, listening, observing or experimenting. Secondly, seek to surround yourself with diversity, people and ideas, because diversity is an inexhaustible reservoir of innovation and creativity. What's more, it's crucial to regularly confront one's own limits, to get out of one's comfort zone, because it's in adversity and challenge that man often finds his greatest strength.

The **16th Commandment** is not just a call to action. It's a philosophy of life, a reminder that evolution is intrinsic to our nature. It urges us to be on a perpetual quest for improvement, to embrace each day as an opportunity to learn, to live fully and to progress.

In an age when information circulates at dizzying speed, technology disrupts our lives and global challenges demand innovative solutions, following this commandment becomes imperative. **Learn, live,**

evolve - three words, one compass for a life rich in meaning and discovery.

The journey of evolution is never-ending. It's a path paved with obstacles and challenges, but also with joys, discoveries and triumphs. By embracing this journey, by staying true to the 16th Commandment, we don't just live. We **blossom**, we **transcend**, and we constantly **evolve.**

> *"Stay evolving, because in the ceaseless flow of progress, those who boldly transform themselves are the ones who draw the contours of the future."*

17th Commandment: Thou shalt challenge thyself!

The humility of knowledge: The odyssey of questioning

In the vast universe of knowledge, where illumination and clarity often coexist with the shadows of ignorance, one truth stands out with dazzling clarity: true wisdom lies in recognizing our limits. Questioning **is a weapon of massive progress**. It's the inner voice that reminds us that, no matter how deep our expertise or how vast our knowledge, there's always an unexplored frontier, an unimagined perspective, an unperceived idea.

Every civilization, every culture and every illustrious thinker who has walked this earth has contributed to the edifice of human knowledge. Yet none of them has dared to proclaim that they have learned everything, understood everything. And why not? Because knowledge is an ocean with infinite horizons, and each wave, each current, offers a new perspective, a new revelation. So **the 17th Commandment** is not just a directive, it's a philosophy of life, an incentive to intellectual humility and perpetual exploration.

When we adopt a posture where we **don't think we know everything**, we open our minds to the infinite potential of learning. This posture protects us from arrogance, complacency and the confirmation trap, the human tendency to seek out and interpret information in a way that confirms our pre-existing beliefs.

However, this awareness is not always easy. We live in a competitive world, where showing signs of weakness or uncertainty can sometimes be perceived as a handicap. But is this really the case? History shows us that the greatest thinkers, from Socrates to Einstein, were those who constantly **questioned** themselves. They were the ones who braved the storms of controversy, who sought answers where others saw only dogma.

It is, of course, tempting to lock ourselves into the fortress of our established beliefs, to ignore dissenting voices and seek security in the comfort of what we already know. However, it is precisely this attitude that can stagnate our personal and intellectual growth. To **step out of our comfort zone is to** embrace the unknown, to challenge our presuppositions, to invite constructive doubt into our quest for truth.

The exercise of questioning, though it may seem trying, offers a treasure trove of benefits. It nurtures our **personal and professional development** by sharpening our critical thinking, broadening our horizons and preparing us to navigate a complex, interconnected world.

To begin this quest, we need to adopt active strategies. **Asking questions**, not only of others, but above all of ourselves, is one of the most effective methods. Seeking to understand, rather than simply to know, takes us to deeper levels of understanding. **Actively listening to** other perspectives, immersing ourselves in disciplines different from our own, and seeking to understand rather than judge, are all powerful tools.

The **17th Commandment** is a compass that guides us towards a life of continuous learning. By following its precept, we recognize that, in the ocean of knowledge, we are mere travelers, sailing from discovery to discovery, seeking to understand and wonder.

Because, in the end, it's not the quantity of what we know that defines our wisdom, but the quality of our curiosity and the depth of our humility. **Don't think you know everything**, but always seek to know more, to understand more, and to embrace the wealth of human knowledge with an open heart and an eager mind.

> *"To question oneself is to open the doors to personal growth; it is in self-questioning that the seeds of wisdom germinate."*

18th Commandment: Thou shalt act as a unifier!

Manifesto of collective power: Human synergy

The timeless proverb: United we stand, divided we fall

Human history is a mosaic of feats, not only of the individual, but above all of the collective. Throughout the ages, vast empires have been built, revolutions have been waged, uncharted heights have been reached, largely thanks to the unified force of the masses. And while the adage **"strength lies in unity"** may seem simple on the surface, at its heart it hides a profound truth about the very nature of our existence.

Within this slide show of collective achievement, the **18th Commandment** stands like a beacon, reminding everyone of the vital essence of unity and mutual support. It underlines that, despite our superficial differences and individual ambitions, we are intrinsically linked by the invisible threads of human destiny. It is by **federating**, by channeling these forces towards a common goal, that we have the potential to transcend the limits of individualism to create something greater than the sum of its parts.

Imagine the professional world without the synergy of a **team**. Projects would be laborious, vision would be narrow, solutions would be one-dimensional. Teamwork is like a dance, where each member brings his or her own cadence, their own style, but all move in harmony towards a common melody. This ability to effectively distribute tasks, to utilize the **diversity of** each individual's **skills**, amplifies our collective capacity to meet challenges and realize bold visions.

But what underpins this collective strength? The glue that holds this fortress together is **mutual aid**. The simple act of reaching out to another, not out of charity but out of solidarity, creates a web of interdependence. These altruistic acts build trust and unshakeable solidarity, forging a community where each member knows he or she is never truly alone.

However, union is not just the coming together of individuals. It can be a collaboration between diverse groups, communities or nations. Think of **social movements**, NGO coalitions, diplomatic alliances. These unifications, motivated by causes greater than themselves, have the power to bring about tangible change, influence policy and inspire generations.

Yet, while advocating union, it is imperative to remember that it must not become a crucible of uniformity. Union must not eclipse **singularity**. Every voice, every nuance, every perspective is essential to creating a rich, vibrant tapestry. Differences shouldn't be dividers, but enrichers, fueling creativity and stimulating innovation. A true union recognizes every color, every tone, while painting a beautiful, coherent picture.

Union is strength, not the oppression of difference, but the celebration of it. It's a call to harmony, not homogeneity. At a time when divisions seem to be growing, the 18th Commandment reminds us that it is only by standing side by side, valuing each individuality, building bridges of mutual understanding, that we can truly move forward.

As humanity moves into the future, it would be wise to meditate on this commandment. For, together, we are truly stronger, more resilient and, without doubt, infinitely more capable of achieving miracles. So let's choose to unite, collaborate and celebrate the beautiful melody of human diversity.

> *"Acting as a federator means weaving together the threads of unity; it's by bringing forces together that we build bridges towards grand designs."*

19th Commandment: Thou shalt not be manipulated!

The Mechanics of Manipulation: Navigating the art of persuasion with wisdom and discernment

At the heart of our journey through life, making decisions, big or small, shapes our existence. And while some decisions may seem trivial, others can have irreversible consequences. The **19th Commandment serves as an** essential compass, guiding us through this complex maze of choices.

Haste is often the enemy of good judgment. Like a work of art requiring hours of attention and finesse, every decision deserves careful consideration. **Wisdom**, that oft-celebrated and sometimes misunderstood quality, is not simply a treasure accumulated over time, but a methodical, considered approach to the turbulent sea of uncertainty.

In this age of information overload, it's imperative to remember that we're all at the mercy of **manipulation**. Insidious manipulation can creep into our lives under many masks: sweet promises from a friend, subtle insinuations from a family member, or even professional pressure from colleagues. And, in some cases, strangers with hidden agendas may try to steer our actions and thoughts to their advantage.

But how can we discern manipulation from simple persuasion or well-intentioned advice? Sometimes the signals may be weak, but

vigilance is our ally. Insistence, excessive emotional appeals or the uncomfortable feeling of being pushed in an unwanted direction are all indicators to watch out for.

Education and the active **search for** information are important safeguards against manipulation. By asking questions, soliciting outside viewpoints and critically evaluating information, we forge a solid defense against attempts to derail us. Trusting our **intuition**, that often overlooked sixth sense, can also serve as a guide when crucial decisions are at hand.

It's natural to ask: why would someone want to manipulate us? Motivations can be many, ranging from a desire for personal gain to a quest for control or influence. Discerning these motivations can not only help us understand the opposing party's intentions, but also counter their strategy.

Strategies can be adopted to ward off manipulation. Questioning, demanding proof, or trying to empathize to understand the other person's point of view, are all approaches to staying in control of your ship in the face of the waves of manipulation.

The ability to say "no" is also a **strength**. In our quest for harmony and social acceptance, we sometimes forget that refusing, setting limits, is not only a right, but also a necessity to preserve our integrity.

Ultimately, the 19th Commandment reminds us that in this complex dance of human interaction, we must be the masters of our decisions, armed with **wisdom** and discernment. The goal is not simply to resist manipulation, but to sail confidently, informed by knowledge, to a harbor of personal satisfaction and true success.

> *"Don't let yourself be manipulated; be the master of your thoughts and choices, for it is in the authenticity of your spirit that your true strength lies."*

20th Commandment: Thou shalt face thy fears!

The audacity of dreams: How to transcend our fears to reach the heights of our aspirations

Few journeys are more daring than those undertaken to realize our deepest aspirations. **Dreams**, those distant and often hazy visions, stand on the horizon of our existence, arousing wonder and anxiety in equal measure. And yet, what is life if not a series of challenges to be met and dreams to be realized?

At one time or another, everyone is confronted with the **abyss of doubts** and fears. These multi-faceted fears, whether they be anxiety about public speaking, hesitation about entering into a new relationship, or reluctance to change direction in one's career, are ancestral sentinels. They are there to alert us, to protect us from potential threats. But when they become chains, they hinder our momentum, preventing us from touching those stars that are our dreams.

Courage is more than an admirable quality; it's also something we develop by getting to know ourselves better and building up little by little. Here's how we can learn to manage our fears in eight simple steps, using our dreams as a guide:

1. **Identifying your fears**: It's like taking a journey inside yourself to understand what you're really afraid of. Do these fears come from bad experiences or influences around us?

It's important to recognize them clearly.

2. **Accepting our fears**: Realizing that our fears are part of who we are. They are not a sign of weakness, but rather an aspect of what makes us human.

3. **Set attainable goals**: You can't achieve everything at once. By setting small goals, we can feel that we're making progress and gradually overcoming our fears.

4. **Seek support**: You're not alone. Having friends, family or even counselors can make a big difference. They can offer advice, support, or just be there to listen.

5. **Visualizing success**: Imagining what it will be like when you succeed can really motivate you. It's like giving yourself extra energy to keep going.

6. **Take your time**: It's important to rest and recharge your batteries. Patience and perseverance are key.

7. **Stay positive**: Even when things are difficult, try to look on the bright side and believe that everything can work out.

8. **Self-confidence**: The most important thing is to believe in your abilities and potential, despite difficulties and doubts.

By following these steps, we can learn to navigate through our fears with courage, getting closer to our dreams every day.

Every dream, every aspiration is both a challenge and a promise. The challenge of **overcoming our fears**, confronting our doubts; the promise of a radiant future, of personal fulfillment. The key lies in our approach, our ability to transform these fears into springboards, and to see in every obstacle an opportunity for growth. **Dare**, with boldness and conviction, because at the intersection of fear and dream lies the magic of realization.

> *"Face your fears, for it is by looking them in the eye that you will discover that they are the gatekeepers to your true power."*

Conclusion

There are crucial moments in human existence when we are called upon to make decisions and shape our destiny. These moments, which may seem insignificant at first glance, are in fact the pillars on which the thread of our lives rests. In this quest for meaning and direction, one injunction resonates loud and clear: take time. Take the time to reflect, to plunge into the abyss of our consciousness, to extract ourselves from the external tumult to refocus on our own essence.

In these modern times, where speed of execution and immediacy are king, allowing ourselves the luxury of reflection, of listening to ourselves, is more than a necessity - it's an act of **resistance**. Indeed, at every street corner, at every bend in the digital path, voices are raised, claiming to hold the truth, the solution to our worries, the direction to take. But how many of these voices are sincere? How many of them have our fulfillment at heart?

Alas, the shadow of the **manipulator** often lurks behind the gentle whispers of unsolicited advice, the injunctions to act one way rather than another, the mirages of turnkey happiness. These entities, veritable **thieves of dreams**, insidiously intrude into the sanctuary of our aspirations, seeking to divert our trajectory, to substitute their vision for ours, to extinguish the flame that burns within us.

It can be seductive, especially when the winds of life blow violently, to take refuge in the bosom of these apparently benevolent figures. The **temptation** to let oneself be guided, to delegate one's ability to judge, is a pitfall to which many succumb. And yet, what an immense loss it is to relinquish one's own rudder, to hand over the helm of one's ship to a stranger, no matter how charismatic.

Life, in all its dazzling complexity, offers each of us the inalienable right of **freedom**. Freedom to think, to choose, to love, to act according to our own convictions and not according to a script pre-established by others. **To live authentically is to** embrace this freedom, to recognize one's own capacity for discernment, and to assert one's individuality in the face of prevailing conformism.

So, in the perpetual dance of influences and advice, there's one imperative: **remain vigilant**. Vigilance against wolves in sheep's clothing, against mirages that promise the best. Vigilance is the bulwark against **lobotomization**, against the dilution of our essence in the great undifferentiated whole. It is the guardian of our dreams, the sentinel of our authenticity.

Ultimately, each individual is the conductor of his or her own inner symphony. Although external scores may offer seductive melodies, it's up to each individual to compose his or her own music, to mark his or her own cadence, to play his or her own notes with passion and conviction. To **make one's own choices**, to free oneself from the shackles of other people's opinions, is to assert one's right to freedom, to assert one's place in the grand scheme of existence.

Let's never forget that, beyond the tumult, the pressures and the doubts, the most reliable, the most precise compass lies within us. It guides us, unfailingly, towards the shores of our dreams, towards the radiant horizon of our authentic destiny. **Let us listen to it**, with respect and gratitude, for it is the silent song of our soul, the echo of our deepest truth.

Thanks

First of all, I'd like to thank my family and friends for their unfailing support throughout the writing of this book. You were there to encourage me, advise me and support me in difficult times.

I'm glad to have been able to share my ideas and experiences with you, and I hope you've found this book useful and informative.

Once again, many thanks to all of you!

www.ingramcontent.com/pod-product-compliance
Lightning Source LLC
Chambersburg PA
CBHW070202230526
45471CB00002B/776